15 Easy & Irresistible

MATH

Mini-Books

Reproducible, Easy-to-Read Stories and Activities That Invite Kids to Add, Subtract, Measure, Tell Time, and Practice Other Important Early Math Skills

**by Sheryl Ann Crawford
and Nancy I. Sanders**

SCHOLASTIC
PROFESSIONAL BOOKS

New York ❋ Toronto ❋ London ❋ Auckland ❋ Sydney
Mexico City ❋ New Delhi ❋ Hong Kong ❋ Buenos Aires

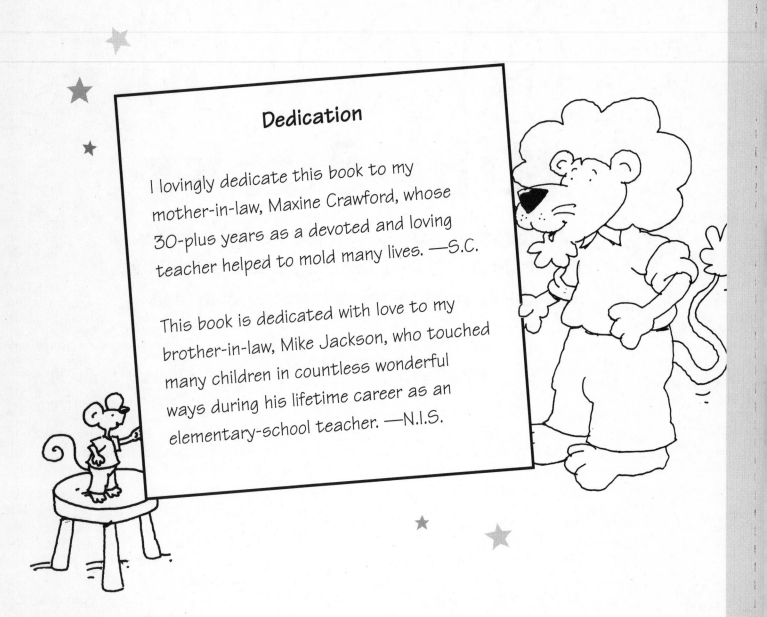

Dedication

I lovingly dedicate this book to my mother-in-law, Maxine Crawford, whose 30-plus years as a devoted and loving teacher helped to mold many lives. —S.C.

This book is dedicated with love to my brother-in-law, Mike Jackson, who touched many children in countless wonderful ways during his lifetime career as an elementary-school teacher. —N.I.S.

Cover design by Weaver Design
Interior design by Grafica, Inc.
Interior illustrations by Patrick Girouard

ISBN 0-439-21612-5
Copyright © 2002 by Sheryl Ann Crawford and Nancy I. Sanders
Printed in the U.S.A.

Table of Contents

Introduction

Understanding how math is incorporated into daily life is a key concept of developmental learning for primary-age children. In *15 Easy & Irresistible Math Mini-Books*, students read stories in which math is used in everyday situations, such as counting seashells at the beach or baking cookies for a birthday party. This reinforces the idea to young children that we are living in a math-oriented world.

These mini-books introduce Lion and Mouse, two lovable and humorous characters who will win the hearts of your students. Predictable language and repetition will help young readers gain confidence practicing their reading skills while strengthening their math skills as they eagerly join Lion and Mouse's math-driven adventures. Children will add the number of falling leaves, measure the size of Lion and Mouse's friends, and watch the clock while cooking Tick-Tock Soup. The last page of each mini-book is a related activity page that reinforces the story's key math concept. Students will take pride in their ability to complete the math activity of the mini-book that they have just finished reading.

An extension activity is included to further reinforce the math concepts in each mini-book. Students learn a rhyme about disappearing crickets as they count backwards from 5. They learn about shapes while cutting out birdhouses for a bulletin-board display. They count to 100 while sharing small surprises from home. Each extension activity is designed to help you provide hands-on reinforcement of the math concepts that were introduced in the mini-books.

The mini-books and their corresponding activities correlate with the standards recommended by the National Council of Teachers of Mathematics (NCTM). A handy chart on page 5 shows how each story and its extension activity connect to the current NCTM Standards.

We hope these funny math mini-books will make your students giggle while sparking their interest in math!

—Sheryl Ann Crawford and Nancy I. Sanders

Connections With the NCTM Standards

	Numbers & Operations	*Estimation	*Number Sense & Numeration	*Concepts of Whole-Number Operations	*Whole-Number Computation	*Fractions & Decimals	Patterns, Functions & Algebra	Geometry & Spatial Sense	Measurement	Data Analysis, Statistics & Probability	Problem Solving	Reasoning & Proof	Communication	Connections	Representation
Lion's Picnic	✾		✾								✾	✾	✾	✾	✾
Counting Shells	✾		✾								✾	✾	✾	✾	✾
100 Birthday Surprises	✾	✾	✾				✾				✾	✾	✾	✾	✾
Adding Leaves	✾		✾	✾	✾		✾			✾	✾	✾	✾	✾	✾
Mouse Has the Hiccups	✾		✾	✾	✾					✾	✾	✾	✾		✾
Five Loud Crickets	✾		✾								✾	✾	✾	✾	✾
Subtraction Cookies	✾			✾	✾		✾			✾	✾	✾	✾	✾	✾
Shapes for the Birds								✾			✾	✾	✾	✾	✾
How Much?	✾		✾							✾	✾	✾	✾	✾	✾
Tick-Tock Soup	✾								✾		✾	✾	✾	✾	✾
Let's Go to the Store!	✾		✾	✾	✾						✾	✾	✾	✾	✾
A New House for Mouse							✾	✾	✾	✾	✾	✾	✾	✾	✾
Lion Likes Patterns							✾					✾	✾	✾	✾
Guess How Many?	✾					✾					✾	✾	✾	✾	✾
Camping Fractions	✾	✾	✾					✾			✾	✾	✾	✾	✾

*Indicates a subcategory of Numbers and Operations.

Extension Activities

Lion's Picnic

Divide the class into small groups. Give each student a lunch-sized paper bag. Place assorted objects on a table. Instruct students to gather small items to put in their bags. Each student should select enough items so that there is one for each member of the group (including themselves).

After students have returned to their groups, ask one student from each group to distribute the objects from his or her bag to the other members of the group. If someone miscounted, let the student go back to get more objects or to return extras. Have students take turns distributing their objects, making sure they give one object to each person. After everyone has had a turn, reorganize the students into different-sized groups and repeat the activity.

HOW TO MAKE THE MINI-BOOKS

1. Make double-sided photocopies of the mini-book pages. Carefully tear along the perforation to remove the pages from the book. (Note: If your photocopy machine does not have a double-sided function, first make copies of mini-book pages 1/3. Place these copies in the paper tray with the blank side facing up. Next, make a copy of mini-book pages 2/4 so that the page copies directly behind pages 1/3. Make a test copy to be sure the pages are aligned correctly and that page 2 appears directly behind page 1. Repeat these steps with pages 5/7 and 6/8.)

2. Cut the mini-book pages apart along the dashed line.

3. Place the pages in numerical order, and then staple them along the mini-book's spine.

4. Invite students to color the illustrations.

6

Counting Shells

Counting along with Lion and Mouse is fun for students as they read this mini-book aloud. Provide each child with 10 counters. As you read each page of the mini-book, allow some time for children to set aside one counter on their desk for each shell Lion finds. (They can place the counters beside their mini-book.) Students can then point to each counter as you read the text aloud and count with Lion.

Challenge students to suggest different numbers of shells for Lion to find. Keep track of these new numbers with the counters. Count up to 20, 50, or more, depending on your students' skill level (and the number of counters on hand!).

100 Birthday Surprises

Prepare for this activity by providing each child with a 5- by 5-inch square of poster board. Have each student take his or her poster board home and glue 10 small items (such as pasta shells, pennies, or candy) onto it. Then have them bring the boards back to class. (Students can do this in class, too.) Ask a few volunteers to stand in line in front of the class and hold up their poster boards. Practice skip counting the objects by tens.

Challenge students to estimate how many more children should join the line to make 100 objects. Bring the suggested number of children forward and continue counting by tens. Was their estimation correct? Discuss the results and continue the activity until 10 children are standing in line. Have students count their objects in unison by tens to get to 100.

Adding Leaves

This mini-book can work hand-in-hand with a quick addition activity. After students have read the mini-book, give them paper, crayons, and scissors to draw and cut out different types of leaves. Each student can make up to ten leaves. When finished, put the leaves in a basket and mix them up.

Ask each student to grab a handful of leaves from the basket. Choose two volunteers to come to the front with their leaves. Ask each one to show his or her leaves to the class and tell how many leaves there are. Then have the pair work together to add the total number of leaves they are holding. Write the number sentence on the board. Repeat the activity with other students to help them build addition skills.

Mouse Has the Hiccups

Photocopy the 10-frame on page 14 for each pair of students. Give each pair counters or markers in two different colors to use on their 10-frame to practice building sums of 10.

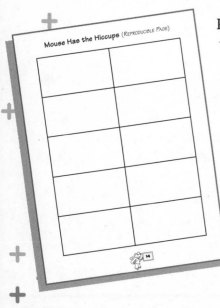

Present students with word problems to make 10, inviting them to use one color for Lion and another for Mouse. For example, Lion and Mouse wanted to pick 10 flowers. Lion picked 6. How many did Mouse pick? Instruct students to keep track of the flowers with their counters. Then ask them to write number sentences based on the word problems.

You can also challenge students to make 10 using more than two numbers. For example, Lion ate 4 hotdogs and Mouse ate 2. How many more hotdogs are left for their friend, Goat?

Five Loud Crickets

Students can act out a simple rhyme while reinforcing counting skills presented in this mini-book. After reading through the story, teach children the following rhyme and motions:

5 loud crickets chirping in the park.

[*Hold up 5 fingers.*]

1 hopped in a hole, where it was cool and dark.

[*Hop and crouch down on the floor, folding down one finger.*]

Now there's only 4 crickets chirping in the park.

[*While crouching, hold up the new number of fingers.*]

Continue the rhyme, counting down each time until "there's only 0 crickets chirping in the park."

Subtraction Cookies

After you have read this mini-book aloud with your class the first time, provide simple manipulatives for them to use when you read it again. Photocopy page 15 for each student and have them cut out the cookies on the page. Give each student a sheet of construction paper to serve as a cookie sheet. Have students place their 10 cookies on their cookie sheets. Now re-read the mini-book. Have students remove cookies from their cookie sheets as Lion eats them.

Encourage students to use the cookies to make up new word problems to share with the class. For example, "Lion baked 8 cookies for the party. He ate 4. How many were left?" Write the number sentences on the board.

Shapes for the Birds

After you have read the mini-book, discuss the different characteristics of each shape. Make photocopies of the birdhouse on page 16 for each student and distribute them. Invite students to pick a shape for the door and draw it on colored paper. Have them cut out their shape and paste it on their birdhouse. Guide students to write, "My door is a triangle (circle, square, or rectangle)" on their house.

Mount the birdhouses in rows on a bulletin board. Label the display "Shapes for the Birds." Use the birdhouses to count and compare the different shapes that children used.

Shapes for the Birds (REPRODUCIBLE PAGE)

How Much?

Before reading this story, ask students to list some standard measuring tools, such as a ruler or yardstick. Explain that you can also use nonstandard tools to measure objects.

After you've read the story, have students measure objects in the classroom with both standard and nonstandard measuring tools, such as paper clips, erasers, or pencils. How many feet long is the chalkboard? How many erasers long is the chalkboard? How many inches long is the eraser? How many paper clips long is the eraser? Encourage students to suggest new tools with which to measure objects around the classroom.

10

Tick-Tock Soup

Work with your class to create a silly recipe for Lion and Mouse to cook, such as meatloaf cookies, jelly-bean pie, or ketchup bread. The recipe should call for an activity—such as stirring the concoction or adding ingredients—once an hour for four hours.

Ask a volunteer to choose a time when Lion and Mouse should start cooking. Show that time on a classroom display clock. Then ask students to figure out the three times for doing the next steps in the recipe. Each time should be exactly one hour after the previous one. Record responses on the board and move the hands on the clock. Repeat with other suggested starting times.

Let's Go to the Store!

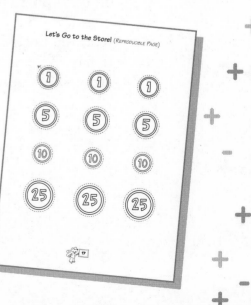

Make enough copies of page 17 so that each child will have at least one coin. Some children will have a penny, others will have a nickel, dime, or quarter.

Display an item from your classroom and assign it an imaginary price of less than one dollar. Ask a volunteer to bring his or her coin and stand in front. Record the coin's value on the board. Ask students whether the coin is too much, too little, or just the right amount to pay for the item. If it's not the right amount, ask volunteers to come forward with their coins to help make the correct amount. Encourage students to work together to get the right combination of coins to pay for the item. Record the results and discuss different possible combinations. When the answer has been determined, display a different item and choose new volunteers to come forward to help make the right amount.

A New House for Mouse

Mouse is moving again! Invite students to sort items for his new house based on the items' characteristics. Photocopy page 18 for each student. Guide them to label each room the same as Mouse's house: big, small, tall, and short. Provide crayons for drawing (or magazines for students to cut out) pictures of items students want to glue in their house.

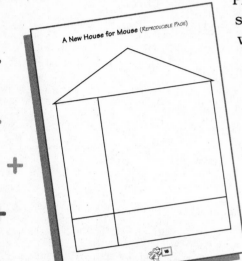

Each item should be put in a different room according to whether it is big, small, tall, or short. Invite students to share their finished pictures. Discuss different characteristics of each item and why it belongs in a certain room.

Lion Likes Patterns

After reading the mini-book, invite children to create new patterns for Lion and Mouse on each page. Write these patterns on the board or on a piece of chart paper. Then read the book again, using the new patterns. Encourage children to say the patterns in unison, or divide the class into different groups, assigning a pattern to each.

Guess How Many?

Divide the class into small groups. Give each group two different-size measuring cups and several samples of one kind of manipulative, such as marbles. Tell the groups to fill one cup with marbles, then count them. Have students write the amount on paper. Encourage students to study the second cup. Ask them to guess how many marbles will fit in this cup. Have each student write down his or her guess. Then count the marbles. Repeat the activity with different types of manipulatives.

Camping Fractions

Fractions are exciting when Lion and Mouse use them! After reading through the mini-book, divide the class into small groups. Give each group a large, rectangular piece of butcher paper and several 4-foot lengths of yarn.

Discuss the different fractions. Draw four rectangles on the board or chart paper. Divide the second one in half, the third one in thirds, and the fourth one in fourths to demonstrate the different fractions. Then ask each group to use their pieces of yarn to divide their butcher paper first into halves, then thirds, and finally fourths. Have students show their work to the other groups.

Mouse Has the Hiccups (REPRODUCIBLE PAGE)

Scholastic • 15 Easy & Irresistible Math Mini-Books

page
14

Subtraction Cookies (REPRODUCIBLE PAGE)

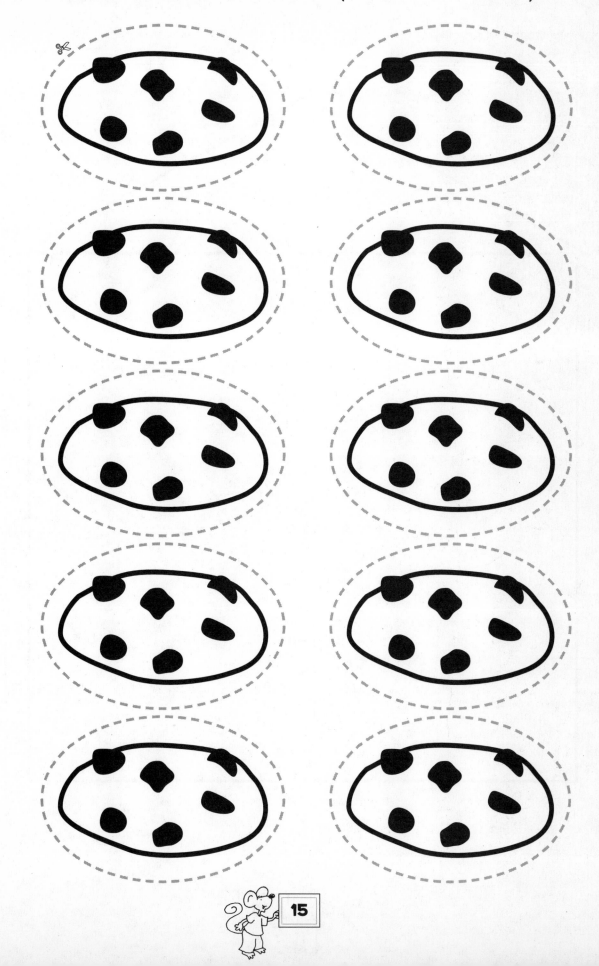

Shapes for the Birds (REPRODUCIBLE PAGE)

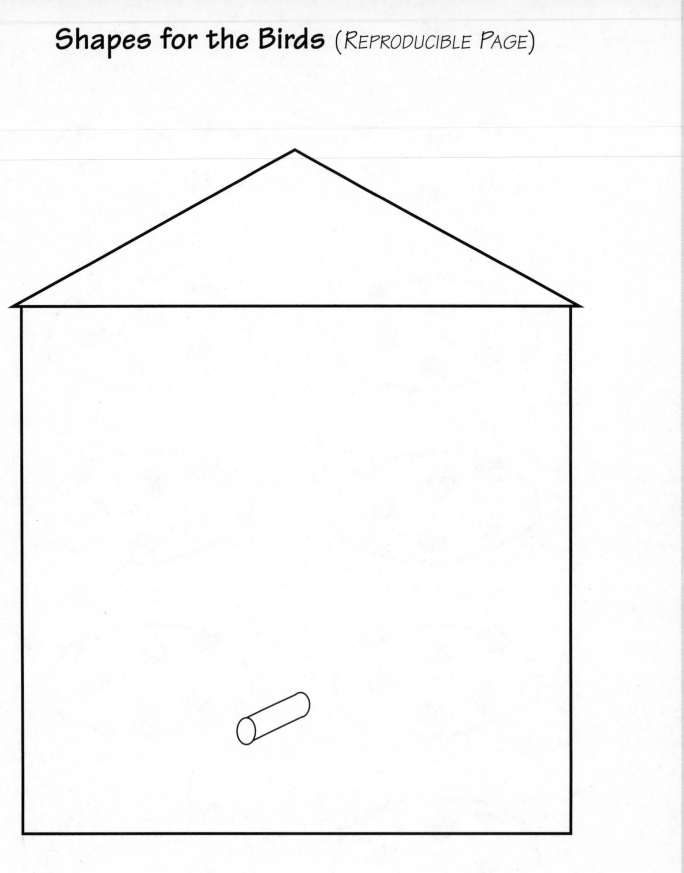

 **16**

Let's Go to the Store!

A New House for Mouse (REPRODUCIBLE PAGE)

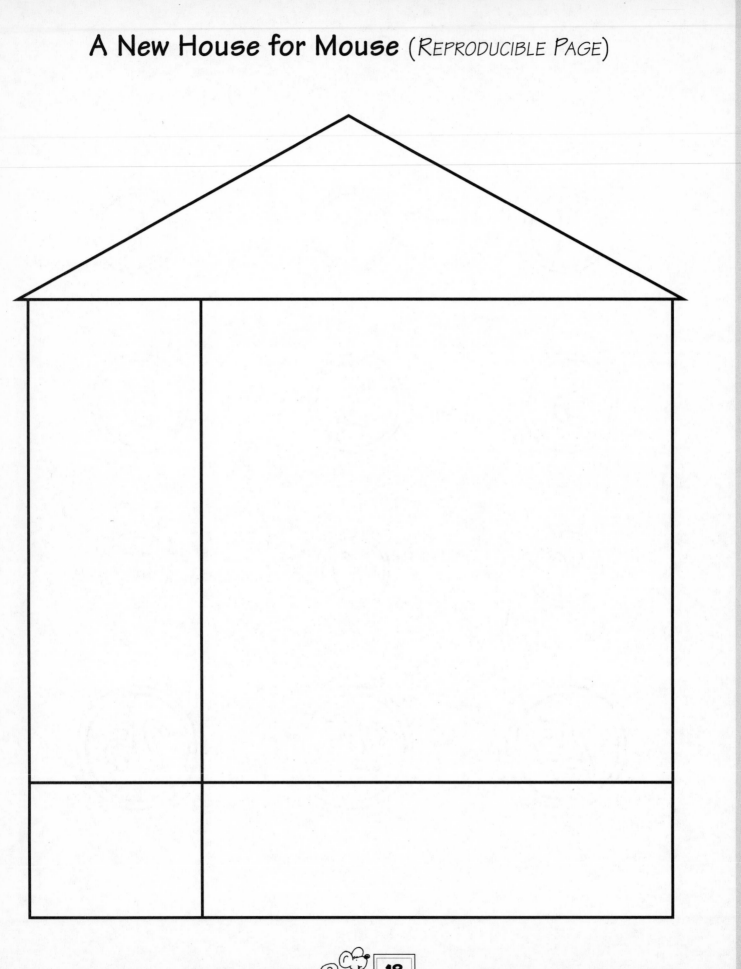

18

THE
MATH
Mini-Books

Welcome to learning math the fun way!

Lion's Picnic

Frog said, "I brought a bag of flies to eat!
There is 1 for each of us."
"Yuck!" cried the friends.

Scholastic • 15 Easy & Irresistible Math Mini-Books

Lion asked his friends to come on a picnic.

2

Goat said, "I brought a bag of rotten apples to eat!
There is 1 for each of us."
"Yuck!" cried the friends.

4

Mouse said, "I brought a bag of stinky cheese to eat!
There is 1 piece for each of us."
"Yuck!" cried the friends.

5

Lion said, "I think we should each eat our own food."
"That is a great idea," said Mouse. "What did you bring?"
"Cookies!" said Lion.
"Not fair!" cried the friends.

7

Bird said, "I brought a bag of worms to eat!
There is 1 for each of us."
"Yuck!" cried the friends.

6

Lion wants to share his cookies.
Draw lines to put one cookie on each plate.

8

COUNTING SHELLS

Lion counted the shells. "One, two, three."
"I'm sitting on a bump," said Mouse.
"More shells?" asked Lion.

"I want to find 10 shells today!" Lion said.
"I want to take a nap," said Mouse.

2

Lion counted the shells. "One, two, three, four, five.
You found the spot with the shells!"
"Lucky me," Mouse said.

4

"Ouch!" cried Mouse. "I was sitting on this shell, too."
Lion counted the shells. "One, two, three, four, five, six, seven, eight."

5

Why me?

"I'm coming with you!" Lion said.
"You know where all the shells are!"

7

"Here's more!" Lion said. He counted the shells.
"One, two, three, four, five, six, seven, eight, nine, and ten!"
"I'm moving to another spot," Mouse said.

6

Count the shells. Draw a ring around the number that tells how many.

2 3 4   7 8 9

8 9 10   5 6 7

Scholastic • 15 Easy & Irresistible Math Mini-Books

100 Birthday Surprises

"Happy birthday, Lion!" said Lion's friends.
"Here are 100 hats for your party."

"Happy birthday, Lion!" said Lion's friends.
"Here are 100 balloons for your party."

2

"Happy birthday, Lion!" said Lion's friends.
"Here are 100 horns for your party."

4

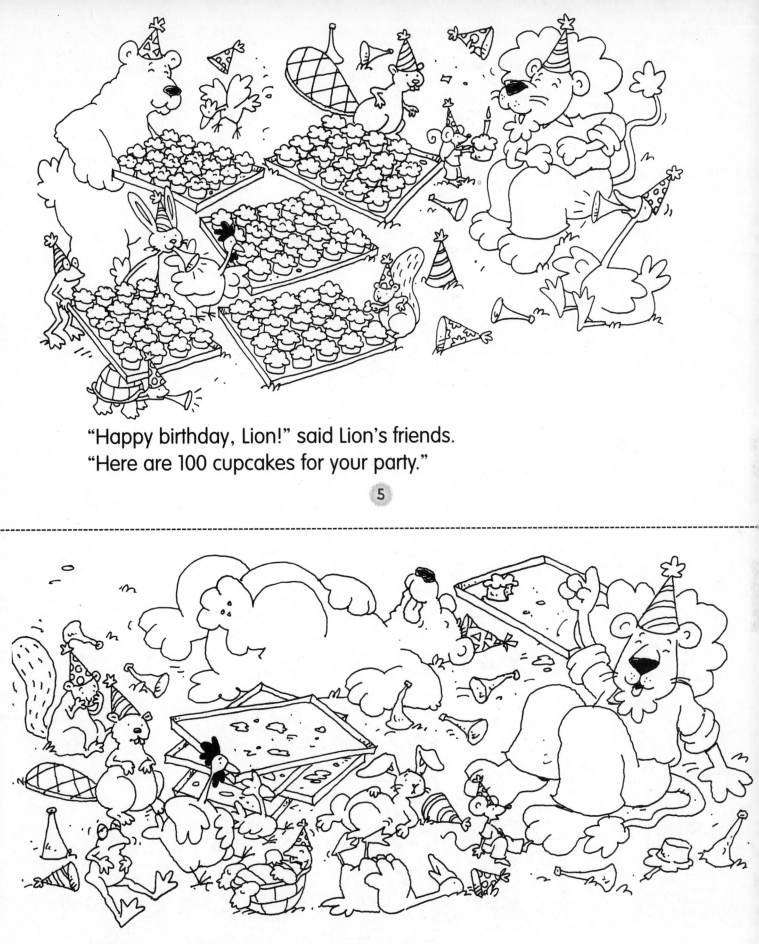

"Happy birthday, Lion!" said Lion's friends.
"Here are 100 cupcakes for your party."

5

"Did you make a wish, Lion?" Mouse asked.
"Yes, I did," said Lion. "I wished for more cupcakes!"

"Happy birthday, Lion!" said Lion's friends.
"Let's sing Happy Birthday 100 times."
"Let's not sing," said Lion. "Let's eat!"

6

Count by ten to reach 100.

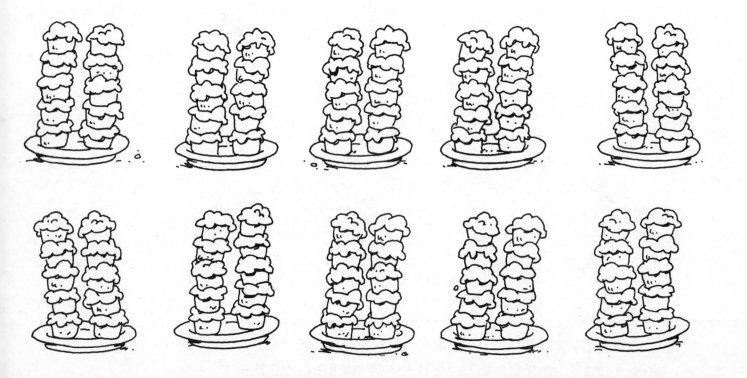

Scholastic • 15 Easy & Irresistible Math Mini-Books

Adding Leaves

"Should I rake the leaves?" asked Lion.
"Yes, you should!" said Mouse. "I will hold the bag."

"I love the fall," Lion said.
"Me too," Mouse said. "Let's add the falling leaves."
They added together.
"2 leaves plus 4 leaves equals 6 leaves."

"Look! More falling leaves," Lion said.
Lion and Mouse added together.
"5 leaves plus 2 leaves equals 7 leaves."

Lion said, "I'll rake them up."
Mouse said, "I'll hold the bag."

"Should we rake them or count them?" Lion asked.
"Let's jump in them!" said Mouse.

"Look! More falling leaves," Mouse said.

6

Add. Write the answers.

$$4 + 2$$

$$5 + 2$$

Scholastic • 15 Easy & Irresistible Math Mini-Books

page 36

Mouse Has the Hiccups

6 + 4 = 10

HIC! HIC! HIC! HIC!

Mouse hiccuped 4 more times.
"Wow!" Lion said. "You hiccuped 10 times!"

Mouse hiccuped 6 times.
Lion gave Mouse a drink of water.

2

Mouse hiccuped 3 times.
"Hold your breath!" Lion said.

4

Mouse hiccuped 7 more times.
"Wow!" Lion said. "You hiccuped 10 times again!"

5

Now Mouse's hiccups are gone!

"ROAR!" Lion shouted. Mouse said nothing.

"Meow," Lion whispered.

"Yikes!" yelled Mouse.

6

Lion and Mouse like to make 10.

Lion picked 6 apples. Mouse picked ____ apples.

$$6 + \rule{2cm}{0.4pt} = 10$$

Scholastic • 15 Easy & Irresistible Math Mini-Books

Five Loud Crickets

"There are four loud crickets in my house!" said Mouse.
"I will catch them one by one."

"There are five loud crickets in my house!" said Mouse.
"I will catch them one by one."

"There are three loud crickets in my house!" said Mouse.
"I will catch them one by one."

Scholastic • 15 Easy & Irresistible Math Mini-Books

"There are two loud crickets in my house!" said Mouse.
"I will catch them one by one."

5

"There are no more loud crickets in my house!" said Mouse.
"Now I can get some sleep."

7

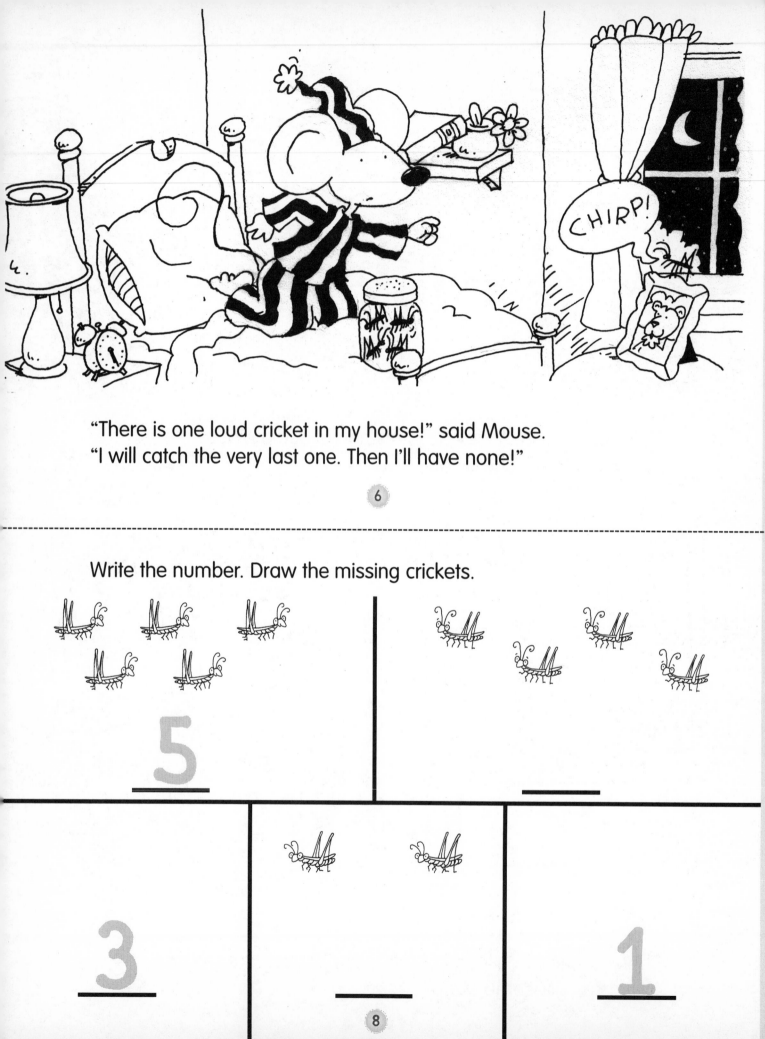

"There is one loud cricket in my house!" said Mouse.
"I will catch the very last one. Then I'll have none!"

6

Write the number. Draw the missing crickets.

5

___

___

3

___

8

___

1

SUBTRACTION COOKIES

Mouse asked, "Did you bake 10 cookies?"
"Yes, I did!" Lion said. "But I ate 3."

"Today is Bird's birthday," Mouse said. "I will bake a cake for the party."
Lion said, "I will bake 10 cookies."

2

"I think 7 cookies are enough for the party," Mouse said.
"Do not eat any more!"

4

"What is that crunching noise?" asked Mouse.
"Did you eat more cookies?"
"I ate 5 more," Lion said. "I am a great cook!"

5

"That's okay," Mouse said. "I have enough cake for everyone."
"Hooray!" said Lion. "And I have enough cookies for 2 friends!"

"Two cookies are not enough for Bird's party," Lion said.

6

Subtract. Write the answers.

Scholastic • 15 Easy & Irresistible Math Mini-Books

page 48

Shapes for the Birds

"What about a square door?" Mouse asked.
"Squares have 4 equal sides," Lion said.

"What is missing from my birdhouse?" Lion asked.

"It needs a round door," said Mouse.

"A circle is round," Lion said.

2

"What about a rectangle?" Mouse asked.

"Rectangles have four sides. Two of the sides are longer," Lion said.

4

Scholastic • 15 Easy & Irresistible Math Mini-Books

"What about a triangle?" Mouse asked.
"A triangle has 3 sides," Lion said.

5

"I hope you like birds!" Mouse said.

7

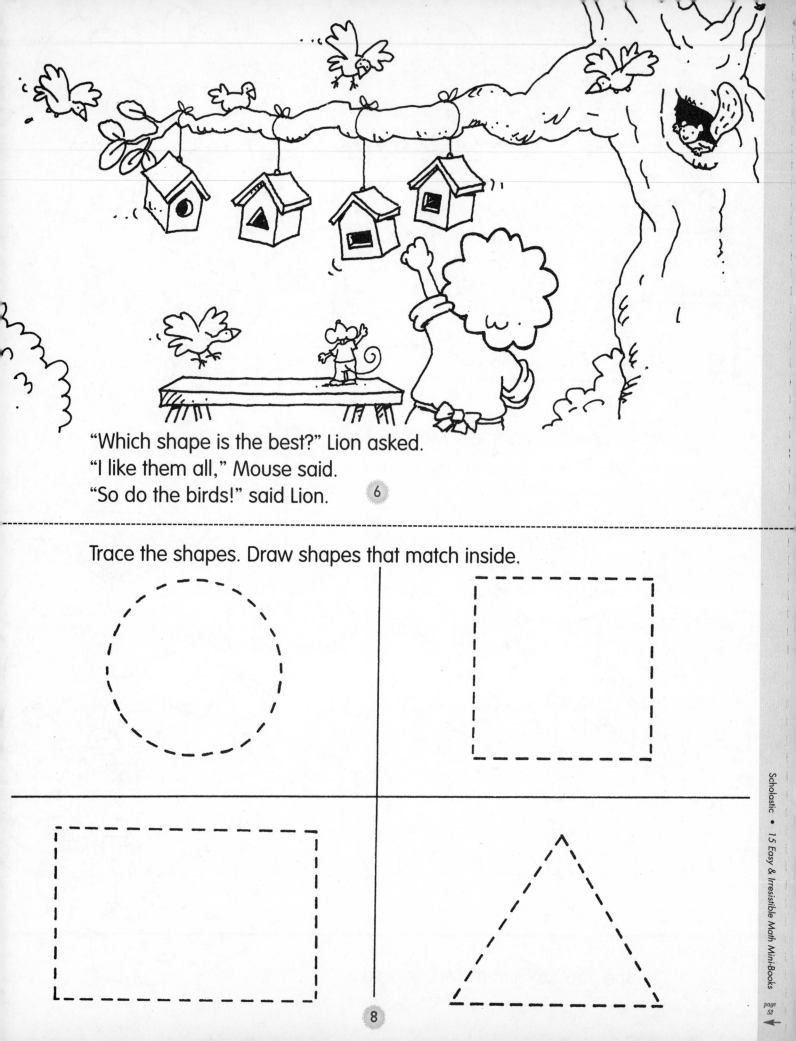

"Which shape is the best?" Lion asked.

"I like them all," Mouse said.

"So do the birds!" said Lion.   6

Trace the shapes. Draw shapes that match inside.

Scholastic • 15 Easy & Irresistible Math Mini-Books

How Much?

"How tall is Cow?" Mouse asked.
"As tall as 10 milk cartons," Lion said.

"How long is Snake?" Mouse asked.
"As long as 5 ham sandwiches," Lion said.

2

"How wide is Frog?" Mouse asked.
"As wide as 3 cookies," Lion said.

4

"How high is your door?" Mouse asked.
"As high as 9 carrots," Lion said.

5

"I don't know about you," Mouse said. "But I am very hungry. Let's eat!"
"Why didn't I think of that?" Lion said.

7

"How heavy is baby Pig?" Mouse asked.
"As heavy as 7 apples," Lion said.

6

How long are Spider and Fish? Count the grapes and shells.

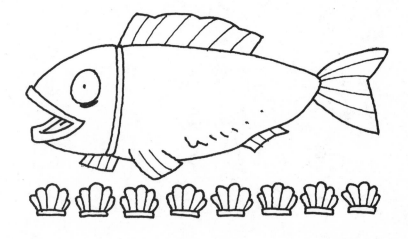

_____   _____

8

Tick-Tock Soup

"It is 9 o'clock. Time to stir the soup," Lion said.
"I'll put in jelly beans, too!"

"We have to stir the soup every hour," Lion said.
"It will be ready to eat in 4 hours," Mouse said.

2

"It is 10 o'clock. Time to stir the soup," Mouse said.
"I'll put in pickles, too!"

4

"It is 11 o'clock. Time to stir the soup," Lion said.
"I'll put in ice cream, too!"

5

"Let's give this soup to Goat," Lion said.
"Yes," Mouse said. "Goat loves homemade soup!"

7

"It is 12 o'clock. Our Tick-Tock Soup is ready!" Mouse said.
"Yuck!" Lion said.
"Ick!" Mouse said.

6

Write the time. Draw the hands.

One hour earlier is ____ o'clock.

It is ____ o'clock.

One hour later is ____ o'clock.

Let's Go to the Store!

"I will buy a toy for 7 cents!" Lion said.
"I don't know what to buy," Mouse said.

3

"I will buy candy for 4 cents!" Lion said.
"I don't know what to buy," Mouse said.

2

"I will buy popcorn for 16 cents!" Lion said.
"I don't know what to buy," Mouse said.

4

Lion and Mouse walked home. "Uh-oh!" Lion said.
"Don't move," said Mouse. "I'll be right back."

5

"Thanks!" Lion said. "You're a great friend!"

"I would like to buy the purse for 28 cents," Mouse said.
"It is a present for my friend."

6

Color the coins to show how much Lion spends.

8

A New House for Mouse

"This is a big room," Lion said.
"Let's put big things in here," Mouse said.

3

Mouse asked, "Lion, will you help me move into my new house?"
"Yes," Lion said. "But where will we put all your stuff?"

2

"Here is a small room," Lion said.
"Small things go in here," Mouse said.

4

"Here is a tall room," Lion said.
"Tall things go in here," Mouse said.

5

"Now your house is full," Lion said.
"Where will I put everything else?" Mouse cried.
"In my room!" Lion said.

7

Scholastic • 15 Easy & Irresistible Math Mini-Books

"Here is a short room," Lion said.
"Short things go in here," Mouse said.

6

Draw a line from each item to the shelf where it belongs.

8

Lion Likes Patterns

"I like patterns when it rains," Lion said.
"I'm not sure I do," Mouse said.

ZIP ZIP BUTTON BUTTON ZIP ZIP BUTTON BUTTON

"I like patterns when I get dressed," Lion said.

2

YAWN YAWN ZZZZ YAWN YAWN ZZZZ

Tick Tick Tick Tock Tick Tick Tick Tock

"I like patterns when I take my nap," Lion said.
"You really like naps, too!" Mouse said.

4

GROWL... HOOT HOOT   GROWL HOOT HOOT

"I like patterns when we go camping," Lion said.
"I'm not sure I do," Mouse said.

5

"I like patterns when I go to bed," Lion said.
"Me, too," Mouse said. "Good night. Sleep tight."

7

"I like patterns when we eat," Lion said.
"I do, too!" Mouse said.

6

Continue the patterns.

Scholastic ● 15 Easy & Irresistible Math Mini-Books

"Now let's count!" Mouse said.

Mouse said, "Four blocks fit in this box."
Lion said, "Guess how many blocks fit in this box?"

2

Mouse said, "Three tennis balls fit in this can."
Lion said, "Guess how many tennis balls fit in this can?"

4

"Now let's count!" Mouse said.

5

"Where are you going?" Mouse asked.
"To find a bigger plate!" Lion said.

7

Mouse said, "Six donuts fit in my plate."
Lion said, "Guess how many donuts fit in my plate?"

6

Count how many pencils are in Lion's box.
Guess how many pencils fit in Mouse's box.

Lion's Box

Mouse's Box

8

Camping Fractions

"Let's divide the tent into two equal parts," Mouse said.
"One half is for me and my things," Lion said.
"One half is for me and my things," Mouse said.

"Our tent is too crowded!" Lion and Mouse said.

2

"It's still too crowded!" Lion and Mouse said.

4

"Let's divide the tent into three equal parts," Mouse said.
"One third is for me," Lion said. "One third is for you."
Mouse said, "And one third is for our things."

5

"Let's divide the tent into four equal parts," Mouse said.
"One fourth is for my things," Lion said. "And one fourth is for your things."
Mouse said, "One fourth is for me. And one fourth is for you."
Good night!

7

"It is still too crowded!" Mouse said. "And I can't see you!"
"That is too bad," said Lion. "I am wearing a funny hat."

6

Draw a circle around the correct fraction.

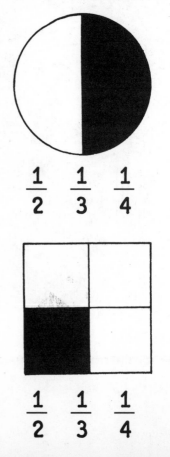

$\frac{1}{2}$ $\frac{1}{3}$ $\frac{1}{4}$

$\frac{1}{2}$ $\frac{1}{3}$ $\frac{1}{4}$

$\frac{1}{2}$ $\frac{1}{3}$ $\frac{1}{4}$

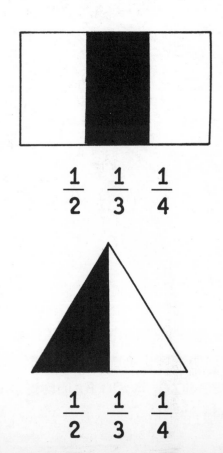

$\frac{1}{2}$ $\frac{1}{3}$ $\frac{1}{4}$

Scholastic • 15 Easy & Irresistible Math Mini-Books

page 80

From the Editors at Scholastic Professional Books

Dear Reader,

We're always delighted when teachers say, "Your books are the ones we use . . . the ones that go to school with us for a day's work . . . the ones that go home with us to help in planning. . . ."

Your comments tell us that our books work for you—supporting you in your daily planning and long-range goals, helping you bring fresh ideas into your classroom, and keeping you up to date with the latest trends in education. In fact, many Scholastic Professional Books are written by teachers, like you, who work in schools every day.

If you have an idea for a book you believe could help other teachers in any grade from K–8, please let us know! Send us a letter that includes your name, address, phone number, and the grade you teach; a table of contents; and a sample chapter or activities (along with color photos, if you have them), to:

Manuscript Editor
Scholastic Professional Books
557 Broadway
New York, NY 10012

Please include a self-addressed, stamped envelope large enough to hold your materials.

We look forward to hearing from you!

—The Editors

SCHOLASTIC
PROFESSIONAL BOOKS

SCHOLASTIC

15 Easy & Irresistible
MATH
Mini-Books

Kids will love reading about Lion and Mouse, two charming characters who embark on math adventures and help build basic skills, such as counting, sorting, estimating, adding, subtracting, and more. Each reproducible mini-book comes with an activity page that reinforces the story's key math concept, plus a super-fun extension activity. A great way to build fluency, practice math skills, and meet the NCTM standards!

Other Books of Interest

Collaborative Math Books For Your Class to Make & Share!
Grades K–2
ISBN: 0-590-64192-1

15 Irresistible Mini-Plays For Teaching Math
Grades K–2
ISBN: 0-439-04386-7

Adding Alligators and Other Easy-to-Read Math Stories
Grades 1–2
ISBN: 0-439-24984-8

ISBN 0-439-21612-5
01295>
UPC
0 78073 21612 3

ISBN: 0-439-21612-5
Price: U.S. $12.95

SCHOLASTIC
PROFESSIONAL BOOKS

Scholastic Inc., 2931 East McCarty Street, Jefferson City, MO 65102